Ten Poems
about Birds

ex libris

Candlestick Press

Published by:
Candlestick Press,
Diversity House, 72 Nottingham Road, Arnold, Nottingham UK NG5 6LF
www.candlestickpress.co.uk

Design and typesetting by Diversity Creative Marketing Solutions Ltd.,
www.diversity.agency

Printed by Ratcliff & Roper Print Group, Nottinghamshire, UK

Selection and Introduction © Katharine Towers, 2017

Cover illustration © Cathy King, 2015

Candlestick Press monogram © Barbara Shaw, 2008

© Candlestick Press, 2017
Reprinted 2018

Donation to The Owls Trust www.theowlstrust.org

ISBN 978 1 907598 51 7

Acknowledgements:

The poems in this pamphlet are reprinted from the following books,
all by permission of the publishers listed unless stated otherwise.
Every effort has been made to trace the copyright holders of the
poems published in this book. The editor and publisher apologise if
any material has been included without permission or without the
appropriate acknowledgement, and would be glad to be told of anyone
who has not been consulted. Thanks are due to all the copyright holders
cited below for their kind permission:

Elizabeth Bishop, *The Complete Poems* 1926-1979 (Farrar, Straus and
Giroux, 1983), by permission of A. M. Heath

Paul Farley, *The Ice Age* (Picador, 2002)

Rebecca Goss, *The Anatomy of Structures* (Flambard Press, 2010) by
kind permission of the author

Kathleen Jamie, *The Tree House* (Picador, 2004)

Michael Longley, *Snow Water* (Jonathan Cape, 2004)

George MacBeth, *A Doomsday Book* (Scorpion Press, 1965) copyright
(c) George MacBeth, 1965. Reproduced by permission of Sheil Land
Associates Ltd.

Katrina Porteous, *The Lost Music* (Bloodaxe Books, 1996)

Lynne Wycherley, *At the Edge of Light* (Shoestring Press, 2003)

Where poets are no longer living, their dates are given.

Introduction

Most birds are shy creatures; they flit across our lives often only half-seen, more often heard. Perhaps this elusiveness is part of their fascination.

This is our second edition of poems about birds and we hope you will be equally delighted by this revised selection. In poems old and new, we're granted an audience with a whole range of birds – from Rebecca Goss's lovesick pigeon to Elizabeth Bishop's nervy sandpiper.

Swallows, swans, an owl, a whitethroat and a snipe rub shoulders with poems exploring what birds represent to us – including Emily Dickinson's mysterious and moving equation of hope with a bird singing in bad weather.

At the centre of the selection, Paul Farley's poem reflects on how birdwatching can seem to encompass a whole life. The speaker's stowaway copy of *A Field Guide to the Birds of Britain & Europe* – a familiar volume for many readers, surely – becomes 'an index of wishful thinking', a testament to the passage of time and to habitats that haven't been visited but are vivid in the imagination.

Reading this selection reminds us that poetry can often achieve at least as much as a pair of binoculars – bringing the extraordinary lives of birds into focus and revealing the intensity and vividness of their worlds. John Clare – perhaps the greatest of all British poets of birds – is acute and tender in equal measure in his observation of the song and behaviour of a whitethroat.

The poet Geoffrey Hill wrote about how a bird will take off *against the wind* to get more purchase on the air. He compares this 'lyric flight' to the writing of a poem in which language works against the grain to capture an experience or a moment. These exquisite poems do just that – fixing the beauty and mystery of birds in our minds for ever.

Katharine Towers

Skylark

Suddenly above the fields you're pouring
Pure joy in a shower of bubbles,
Lacing the spring with the blue thread of summer.
You're the warmth of the sun in a song.

You're light spun to a fine filament;
Sun on a spider-thread –
That delicate.

You're the lift and balance the soul feels,
The terrible, tremulous, uncertain thrill of it –
You're all the music the heart needs,
Full of its sudden fall, silent fields.

Katrina Porteous

Pigeon Love

I know he sweats in his bed about me.
Nights before races are longest,
as he dreams of the money my feathers
can make him, sees my eager beak pointing

towards home. Nights like this are hard for me too,
caging us together, my love and I,
leaving me to nudge her plumy neck,
peck that secret part beneath her wing.

He relies on *widowhood* to get me back,
simple but it works. Passion, sex, comfort
being parted from all that, makes me fly faster,
guarantees I'm a winner. When that businessman

in Taiwan bet $50,000, did he know he wagered
on mourning and love? At six days old, they punched
a ring on my leg, the number defining my lot,
who I belonged to and he does care for me -

pets me with chubby, tender hands
but she's the one who increases my rapidity,
her softness accelerates swiftness,
lift up your wing, high so I can see, I'm coming home.

Rebecca Goss

*widowhood: term used to describe the period racing pigeons spend apart from
their mate during flights*

Snipe
In memory of Sheila Smyth

I wanted it to be a snipe from Belfast Lough's
Mud flats, the nightflier that jooked into my headlights.
It could as well have been a knot or a godwit
From the Arctic, a bar-tailed godwit would you say?
Oh, what amateur ornithologists we are!
I had been out celebrating your life, and now
Here you were flapping into your immortality.
Everyone who loved you remembers how birdlike
Your body and behaviour were, exquisiteness.
I stopped the car and held in my lights the lost bird.
It froze like an illustration, the sensitive
Long beak disinclined to probe the tarmacadam.

Michael Longley

Owl

is my favourite. Who flies
like a nothing through the night,
who-whoing. Is a feather
duster in leafy corners ring-a-rosy-ing
boles of mice. Twice

you hear him call. Who
is he looking for? You hear
him hoovering over the floor
of the wood. O would you be gold
rings in the driving skull

if you could? Hooded and
vulnerable by the winter suns
owl looks. Is the grain of bark
in the dark. Round beaks are at
work in the pellety nest,

resting. Owl is an eye
in the barn. For a hole
in the trunk owl's blood
is to blame. Black talons in the
petrified fur! Cold walnut hands

on the case of the brain! In the reign
of the chicken owl comes like
a god. Is a goad in
the rain to the pink eyes,
dripping. For a meal in the day

flew, killed, on the moor. Six
mouths are the seed of his
arc in the season. Torn meat
from the sky. Owl lives
by the claws of his brain. On the branch

in the sever of the hand's
twigs owl is a backward look.
Flown wind in the skin. Fine
rain in the bones. Owl breaks
like the day. Am an owl, am an owl.

George MacBeth (1932 – 1992)

Bewick Swans arrive at Ouse Washes

Just when I think the winter has won,
a black book closing

on pages of light,
and the darkness sways on its haunches

like an impatient bear
scooping up silver minnows,

I sense an agitation in the sky,
long Vs trailing like pennons.

Altocirrus, swans white
as the tundra they come from.

Their cries multiply. Their bodies
crash-land on the water

star after star after star.

Lynne Wycherley

The Happy Bird

The happy white throat on the sweeing bough
Swayed by the impulse of the gadding wind
That ushers in the showers of april – now
Singeth right joyously and now reclined
Croucheth and clingeth to her moving seat
To keep her hold – and till the wind for rest
Pauses – she mutters inward melodys
That seem her hearts rich thinkings to repeat
And when the branch is still – her little breast
Swells out in raptures gushing symphonys
And then against her blown wing softly prest
The wind comes playing an enraptured guest
This way and that she swees – till gusts arise
More boisterous in their play – when off she flies

John Clare (1793 – 1864)

Note: this version follows the spelling and grammar given in John Clare, Major Works, OUP, 1984

A Field Guide to the Birds of Britain & Europe

was the first book I owned, not counting annuals,
eighteen volumes of the *New Junior Encyclopaedia*
and an illustrated Bible. I could tick them off
as they occurred: so the starling, blackbird and house sparrow
fell on the first day, though the hoopoe and bee-eater
never blew through the 'wettest summer on record'.

Like a biroed Bede at his illuminations,
the pleasing lines of waders' beaks or raptors' talons
kept me occupied for hours. I wandered its pages
of saltmash, heath and scrub: it was its own landscape
and a codex to the calls that book-ended daylight,
becoming so revised and enlarged in the memory

that, sometimes, birds would bleed beyond their range maps;
so while the chough had pooled like glacial ink
in the Welsh hills, or the nightingale occupied that corner
of England left unscoured by the last Ice Age,
I half-heard a flinty *kwak* or the fluid phrasings
of 'one of our best singers' in a northern twilight.

How it came south I'll never know. A stowaway
in that first case I thumped onto puce candlewick,
camouflaged among the set-texts. I can entertain
the image of it making the round trip
back here, to the city it was printed in,
shedding its dust-jacket like juvenile plumage.

It seems smaller now, an index of wishful thinking.
Look at the notes in the flyleaves – the accidental visitors
and colourful migrations of one, bored summer –
offsetting the world outside my window, as if seen
down the wrong end of those field-glasses from Freemans
which were pawned for something irredeemable.

Paul Farley

"Hope" is the thing with feathers

"Hope" is the thing with feathers –
That perches in the soul –
And sings the tune without the words –
And never stops – at all –

And sweetest – in the Gale – is heard –
And sore must be the storm –
That could abash the little Bird
That kept so many warm –

I've heard it in the chillest land –
And on the strangest Sea –
Yet – never – in Extremity,
It asked a crumb – of me.

Emily Dickinson (1830 – 1886)

Sandpiper

The roaring alongside he takes for granted,
and that every so often the world is bound to shake.
He runs, he runs to the south, finical, awkward,
in a state of controlled panic, a student of Blake.

The beach hisses like fat. On his left, a sheet
of interrupting water comes and goes
and glazes over his dark and brittle feet.
He runs, he runs straight through it, watching his toes.

– Watching, rather, the spaces of sand between them,
where (no detail too small) the Atlantic drains
rapidly backwards and downwards. As he runs,
he stares at the dragging grains.

The world is a mist. And then the world is
minute and vast and clear. The tide
is higher or lower. He couldn't tell you which.
His beak is focussed; he is preoccupied,

looking for something, something, something.
Poor bird, he is obsessed!
The millions of grains are black, white, tan, and gray,
mixed with quartz grains, rose and amethyst.

Elizabeth Bishop (1911 – 1979)

Swallows

I wish my whole battened
heart were a property
like this, with swallows
in every room – so at ease

they twitter and preen
from the picture frames
like an audience in the gods
before an opera

and in the mornings
wheel above my bed
in a mockery of pity
before winging it

up the stairwell
to stream out into the light

Kathleen Jamie